First published 1983 by Editions Gallimard
First published in Great Britain in 1985 by
Moonlight Publishing Ltd,
131 Kensington Church Street, London W8
© 1983 by Editions Gallimard
English text © 1985 by Moonlight Publishing Ltd

Printed in Italy by La Editoriale Libraria

ISBN 1 85103 071 9

Thanks are due to the Royal Greenwich Observatory for its help
with the provision of astronomical data.

THE BOOK OF
THE SKY

DISCOVERERS

by Jean-Pierre Verdet

illustrated by
**Christian Broutin
Christine Adam
Jean-Louis Besson
Isaï Correia
André Rollet**

translated and adapted by
Sarah Matthews

Scientific Adviser: Heather Couper

MOONLIGHT PUBLISHING

Flying

I saw the moon
One windy night,
Flying so fast —
All silvery white —
Over the sky,
Like a toy balloon
Loose from its string —
A runaway moon.
The frosty stars
Went racing past,
Chasing her on
Ever so fast.
Then everyone said,
'It's clouds that fly,
And the stars and moon
Stand still in the sky.'
But I don't mind —
I saw the moon
Sailing away
Like a toy
Balloon.

J.M. Westrup

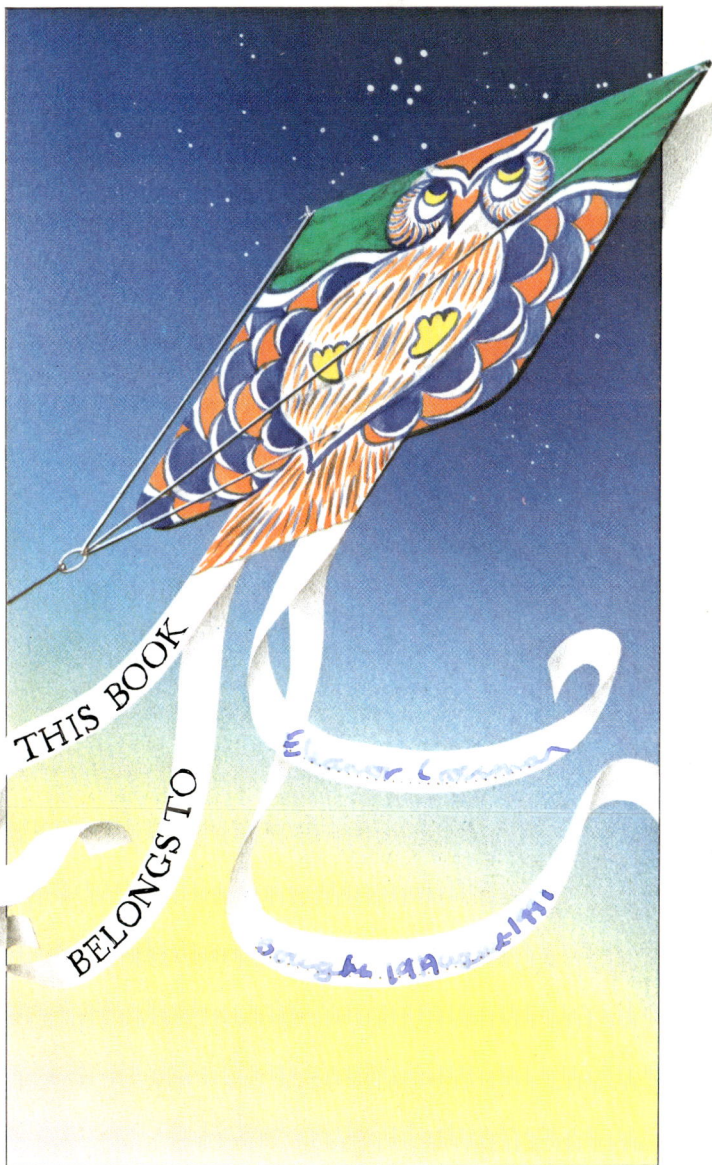

THIS BOOK

BELONGS TO

7

The sky at night

Look up at the sky on a clear evening, as the sun goes down. What do you see?

Sometimes, in the last faint rays of sunlight, before the moon appears, you can make out something glimmering. It is Venus, the third brightest object in the sky (only the sun and moon are brighter). Because it can best be seen at dusk, Venus is also called the evening star. It is not really a star, though, but a planet from our own solar system.

Gradually, as the sky darkens, the true stars become visible. More and more and more of them.

Some seem brighter than others, and make patterns across the sky — *constellations*. If you look at the same constellations, from the same place, at the same time of year, they will appear unchanged. But if you watch them day after day as the year progresses they seem to wheel gently across the sky, and to rotate each night around the Pole Star, the bright fixed point of light which marks the north.

Across the sky stretches a dim, luminous band of light — the Milky Way. In ancient times this was thought to be some sort of steam or fog rising from the Earth.

Now we know that the Milky Way is composed of millions of distant stars. There are so many of them, and they are so far away, that we cannot see them separately with the naked eye. Our Milky Way is a galaxy of stars. It is just one among millions and millions of galaxies, which stretch far out into space – farther than anyone knows.

Our own galaxy is like a sort of Catherine wheel of stars, spinning slowly through space, with our solar system placed about two-thirds of the way out towards the edge. There may be solar systems – planets – around the other stars in the Milky Way.

From the Earth we can look in, towards the heart of our own galaxy, or out, towards the others.

The constellations

The Pole Star is the last star in the tail of the Little Bear. To find it, draw an imaginary line from the last two stars in the Great Bear's chest. The Pole Star is five times as far from the Great Bear as the last two stars in the chest are from each other.

Watching the stars from Earth is like sitting on a train in a station and watching the train alongside yours pull out; for a moment it seems to be your train which is moving. Seen from the Earth, the stars seem to move, but in fact it is the Earth spinning daily on its axis which makes the stars appear to rise and set. The stars seem to move slowly from night to night, too. But this is a result of our year-long orbit around the sun, so that we see the stars from a slightly different position each night. The stars do move – but they are so far away that it takes many human lifetimes for this motion to become noticeable.

The Pole Star seems not to move because it is directly in line with the Earth's axis. But the position of the axis changes slightly each time the Earth revolves.

The Dragon is a constellation made up of 16 stars. You can find it in the star charts on pages 20 to 27.

It takes 26,000 years for the Earth's axis to make a complete circle, and during that time it lines up with different stars. There have been three Pole Stars since astronomical records were first kept. At the moment it is Polaris, or Alpha in Ursa Minor (the Little Bear). Before that, it was Beta in Ursa Minor, and before that a star in the Dragon constellation.

Magnitude

The Giraffe got its name by mistake. Bertschius, the Dutch astronomer, wanted to call it the Camel, after one of the camels that carried Rebecca to Isaac in the Bible. But the name was written down wrongly; instead of being the Greek for camel, it was the Greek for giraffe – and that's what it's been called ever since.

Constellations are groups of stars which look from Earth as if they are arranged in patterns. Not all stars in a constellation are of the same brightness.

Stars are classified by their brightness, or *magnitude*. The magnitude of a star depends on four things: how bright it really is, how big it is, how far away it is, and how hot or cold it is. A very big, hot, bright star far away may appear as bright as a much smaller, fainter star which is closer to us.

For instance, the constellation of the Giraffe, or Camelopardalis, named by a Dutch astronomer in the seventeenth century, is an arrangement of stars between Perseus, Cassiopeia and the Great and Little Bears. The stars in the Giraffe are not really close together, though, they only seem so to us from Earth.

How constellations are named

Ever since astronomers started observing the skies, constellations have been given names.

Perseus is a straggling constellation of 12 stars. One star, Beta Persei, is also called Algol, from the Arabic name *Ras al Ghul*, which means 'Demon's Head'.

Different cultures have given the constellations different names — the Babylonians, the Chinese, the Arabs, all had their own names. The names we use today are Latin, and many are based on the Greek and Roman myths.

For instance, near Ursa Minor, Perseus, the Greek hero, still stands beside Andromeda, the princess he saved and married, while his winged horse, Pegasus, flies alongside them. In another part of the sky, the Lion is supposed to be the skin of a famous lion killed by Hercules and flung up into the sky.

The stars . . .

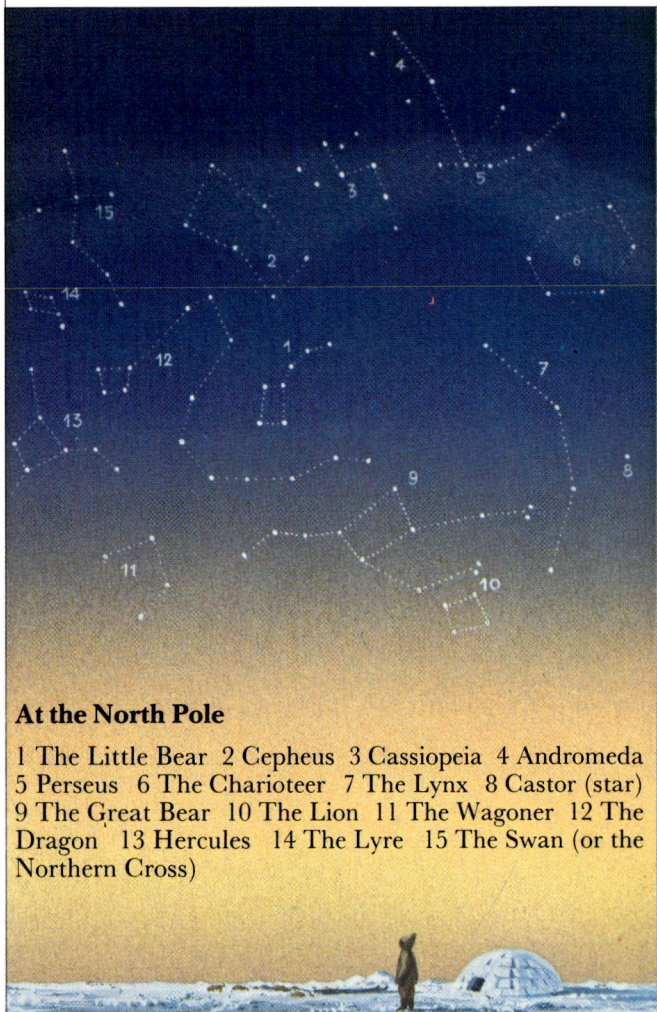

At the North Pole

1 The Little Bear 2 Cepheus 3 Cassiopeia 4 Andromeda
5 Perseus 6 The Charioteer 7 The Lynx 8 Castor (star)
9 The Great Bear 10 The Lion 11 The Wagoner 12 The
Dragon 13 Hercules 14 The Lyre 15 The Swan (or the
Northern Cross)

. . . at the Poles

At the South Pole

1 The Phoenix 2 The Crane 3 The Toucan 4 The Hydra
5 The Peacock 6 The Octant 7 The Southern Triangle
8 The Altar 9 The Scorpion 10 The Wolf 11 The Southern Cross 12 The Sails (of the Ship) 13 The Swordfish
14 The Dove 15 Eridanus 16 The Centaur

The stars . . .

1 Pegasus   2 The Water-carrier   3 The Sea-goat   4 The Fishes 5 The Southern Fish 6 The Swan (or the Northern Cross)   7 The Dolphin   8 The Eagle   9 The Lyre 10 Hercules 11 Ophiuchus 12 The Serpent 13 The Archer 14 The Scorpion   15 The Scales   16 The Virgin   17 The Wagoner   18 The Northern Crown

. . . at the equator

19 The Little Lion   20 The Lion
21 The Hydra   22 The Ship Argo
23 The Great Dog   24 The Unicorn
25 The Little Dog   26 The Crab
27 The Twins 28 Orion 29 The Bull
30 The Charioteer   31 The Pleiades
(or the Seven Sisters)   32 Perseus
33 Andromeda   34 The Ram   35 The
Whale   36 Eridanus 37 The Hare

Stars to steer by

In days before chronometers and reliable compasses, sailors used to navigate by the stars, the sun and the moon. Their position in the sky gave the sailors their direction.

How? The easiest way is obviously to use the rising and the setting of the sun. The sun rises in the east and sets in the west (more or less so throughout the year, and exactly so on 21 March and 23 September). To find the north, you only have to stand with the east on your right and the west on your left.

Another way to find the north by the sun is by using an ordinary clock or watch face (so long as it's not a digital watch . . .). Make sure your watch is set to solar time (British Summer Time is one hour ahead, so set your watch back an hour during spring and summer). Then align the little hand with the sun. If you now take a twig, and divide the angle between the little hand and an imaginary line between the centre of the watch and the numeral 12, the twig will point north-south.

At night, when there was no sun to steer by, sailors used to take their direction from the Pole Star, which stands due north.

Star-gazing

Before you begin star-gazing, you need to know whether you are looking north or south. Until you grow familiar with the constellations, and can pick out the Pole Star directly, the best way to find direction is with a compass. This will show you magnetic north. Geographic north is very slightly to the right of magnetic north, and there you will find the Great Bear and the Little Bear, with the Pole Star in his tail (see p.10).

In the following pages we give you star charts for the different times of year in the northern hemisphere (the stars you see in the southern hemisphere are, of course, rather different). If you can't immediately pick out the constellations shown on these charts from the welter of stars in the sky, you can use the charts to make your own quick guides to the constellations.

Decide which constellation you want to observe, then trace over its diagram on the chart. Lay your tracing over a piece of black card, and prick holes through the positions of the stars so that you have holes right through the card. Now you can hold your card up against the sky until the pattern of stars exactly matches the pattern of holes. You will have found your constellation.

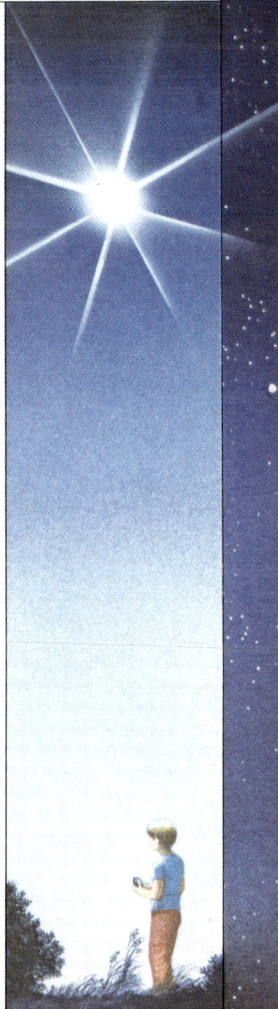

The stars in spring

The name of the Dragon constellation is very old. It goes back to the Babylonians.

In Babylonian myth, when Marduk, their chief god, had vanquished Chaos, he took the body of Tiamat, the great dragon, and split it in two.

With one half he created the Earth, with its valleys, rivers and mountains.

The Dragon

Opposite it, in the sky, Marduk placed the other half, setting in it the sun, the moon and the Pole Star.

Around the Pole Star Marduk arranged the other stars. One particular arrangement he made in the shape of Tiamat: the constellation of the Dragon.

So Tiamat the Dragon was trapped in the heavens for all eternity.

Towards the south

1 The Virgin
2 The Lion
3 Berenice's Hair
4 The Great Bear
5 The Crab
6 The Twins
7 Orion
8 The Great Dog
9 The Hydra
10 The Goblet
11 The Crow
12 The Wagoner

The stars in summer

In the constellation of the Lyre, just above the Milky Way shines a star called Vega.

Just below the Milky Way, in the constellation of the Eagle, shines a star called Altair.

The story goes that Vega is the daughter of a god, while Altair is only a poor cowherd.

The Lyre and the Eagle

But Vega is in love with Altair.

Once a year, on the seventh day of the seventh month, all the crows in the world fly upwards, and make a bridge together in the sky.

And over the bridge Vega creeps silently to meet in secret with her beloved cowherd.

Towards the south

1 The Lyre
2 Hercules
3 Ophiuchus
4 The Crown
5 The Wagoner
6 The Virgin
7 The Scales
8 The Archer
9 The Goat
10 The Water-
    carrier
11 The Fishes
12 Pegasus
13 The Dolphin
14 The Eagle
15 The Swan
16 The Serpent
17 The Scorpion

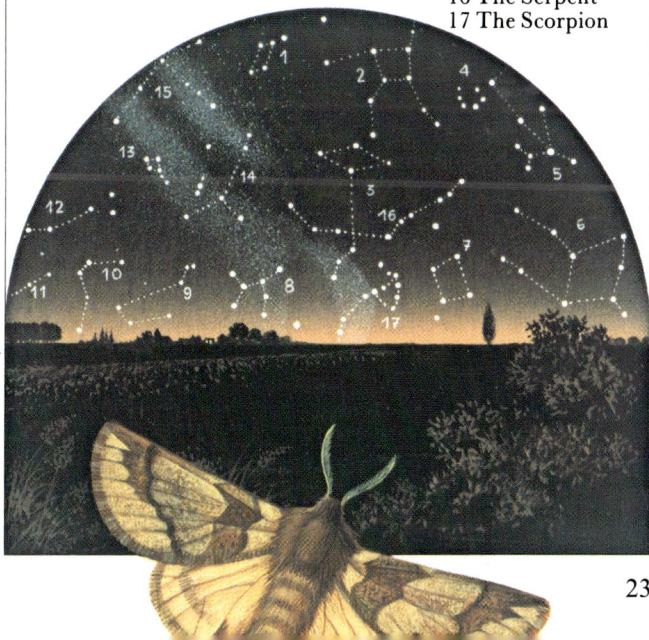

23

The stars in autumn

Towards the north

1 The Little Bear
2 Cepheus
3 Cassiopeia
4 The Dragon
5 Hercules
6 The Crown
7 The Wagoner
8 The Serpent
9 The Great Bear
10 The Charioteer
11 The Bull
12 Perseus
13 The Swan
14 The Lyre

The constellation of the Fishes is very familiar to North American Indians.

It reminds them of the time when, living in the land of eternal winter, they were born with fishes' tails. One day, tired of the perpetual cold, they decided to climb the Great Mountain to get closer to the sky. When they reached the top, one of them leaped up and made a great gash in the sky.

The Fishes

Immediately, warm air began to drift down on to the land of the Fish tribe. When half the warm air had seeped out of the sky, the people of the sky grew angry, killed the chief of the Fish tribe, and slammed shut the rift. When night fell, the Indians saw a new constellation in the sky, the constellation of the Fishes. And ever since then, the Indians have been born without fishes' tails, and have lived in a land that is sometimes cold, and sometimes warm.

Towards the south

1 Pegasus
2 The Dolphin
3 The Water-carrier
4 The Goat
5 The Eagle
6 The Swan
7 Ophiuchus
8 The Archer
9 The Southern Fish
10 The Whale
11 Eridanus
12 The Fishes
13 The Serpent

The stars in winter

If the constellation of the Ram shines so brightly in the sky, it's because God doesn't want us to forget what happened when the Devil defied Him.

One day the Devil wanted to create his own world. So he modelled a ram out of clay. Then he tried to give it life. For two days he circled round the ram, bleating at it and trying to get it to come alive.

The Ram

God watched all this quietly. On the third day He went up to the Devil and asked him what was going on. At first the Devil didn't want to tell God; then he admitted that he'd made the ram, but couldn't get it to come alive. God touched the ram's head and bleated gently at it twice. Immediately the ram began to breathe and, with a toss of its head, trotted off to feed on the nearby bushes. The Devil gazed after it, mortified.

Towards the south

1 Orion
2 The Bull
3 The Pleiades
4 Perseus
5 The Ram
6 The Charioteer
7 Andromeda
8 Pegasus
9 The Fishes
10 The Water-
   carrier
11 The Whale
12 Eridanus

Light

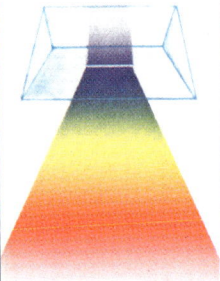

Newton's prism breaks up the light into the colours of the spectrum.

Light travels at 300,000 km a second, yet it takes over four years for light from the nearest star to Earth to reach us. We can only see a small proportion of the stars that are in the sky — some are too faint, some too distant to be visible to the naked eye. The astronomer Sir James Jeans has said that there are as many stars in the universe as there are grains of sand on all the beaches of all the oceans of the world.

The invention of the telescope, which made distant objects appear closer, revolutionised astronomy and made many more stars visible. In December 1609, an Italian called Galileo used the newly-discovered telescope to observe and describe for the first time the mountains of the moon, the satellites of Jupiter and the rings of Saturn.

Galileo

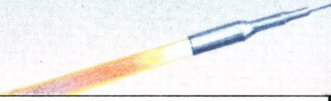

Rainbows At the end of the seventeenth century the English scientist, Sir Isaac Newton, improved the telescope by using mirrors instead of lenses. He also invented a glass prism which broke up the sun's light into the seven basic colours which make it up — the seven colours of the rainbow. This provided astronomers with a way of studying the nature of a star, its chemical composition, its temperature, by looking at the nature of the light which it gives out.

At both ends of the spectrum revealed by Newton's prism there are radiations invisible to the naked eye: at one end, *ultra-violet* (literally, 'beyond violet'), at the other, *infra-red* ('below red').

Most of these radiations do not penetrate the Earth's atmosphere, which extends more than 10,000 km into space. Starting from the Earth's surface, first comes the *troposphere*, the air we breathe. Then, above 10 km, the *stratosphere* with its precious ozone layer to filter out dangerous ultra-violet rays. Next, above 80 km, the highly rarefied *ionosphere*, and finally, at over 10,000 km, the *exosphere*, a layer so thin and loosely bonded that from here the atoms and molecules disperse and escape into infinite space.

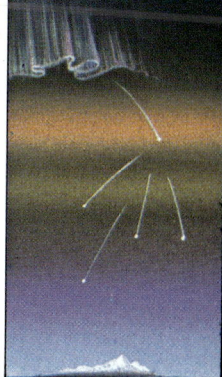

Red giants . . .

Stars are enormous spheres of burning gases. If you look very carefully you can see they are different colours.

Brightness and colour On a July night Vega, in the Lyre constellation, and Arcturus, in the Wagoner, are of about the same brightness, but Vega is bluish while Arcturus appears slightly reddish, because Vega is considerably hotter than Arcturus—about 10,000°C as opposed to about 4,000°C. The hotter stars are, the whiter their light.

Density and mass Stars also differ in *density* and *mass* (weight). Some very small stars can be very heavy — Sirius B is about 100 times smaller than our sun, yet about the same weight – because of the behaviour of their atoms. Ordinarily, every atom is made up of a tiny nucleus surrounded by electrons at a relatively great distance from it; if the nucleus were the size of a marble, then the electrons would be, proportionally, several kilometres away. Each electron is surrounded by a shell which keeps it separate from the others. In white dwarfs, the electrons have lost their shells, and crowd together, making stars of extraordinary density. In some white dwarfs, one cubic centimetre of matter has a mass of one ton.

A red giant, a white dwarf

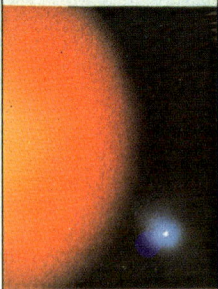

. . . and white dwarfs

Very bright stars:		
Sirius (The Great Dog)		White with yellow dwarf companion
Canopus (The Ship's Keel)		Yellow giant
Alpha Centauri (The Centaur)		System of 3 stars
Arcturus (The Wagoner)		Red giant
Vega (The Lyre)		White
Rigel (Orion)		Blue giant
Capella (The Charioteer)		System of 2 yellow giants
Procyon (The Little Dog)		Yellow with white dwarf companion
Achernar (Eridanus)		Blue
Beta Centauri (The Centaur)		Blue-white
Altair (The Eagle)		White
Aldebaran (The Bull)		Red giant
Acrux (The Southern Cross)		System of 2 blue-white stars
Betelgeuse (Orion)		Red supergiant
Antares (The Scorpion)	Their size and colour	Red supergiant with small green companion

The solar system

The planets and their symbols	Their distance from the sun (in millions of km)	Duration of their revolution around the sun	Duration of their rotation	Their diameter (in km)	Number of satellites
Mercury ☿	58	88 days	58 days	4,900	0
Venus ♀	108	225 days	243 days	12,100	0
Earth ♁	150	365 days	24 hours	12,800	moon
Mars ♂	230	687 days	25 hours	6,800	2
Jupiter ♃	780	12 years	10 hours	143,000	16
Saturn ♄	1,420	29 years	10 hours	120,000	23
Uranus ♅	2,900	84 years	16 hours	51,000	5
Neptune ♆	4,500	165 years	22 hours	49,000	2
Pluto ♇	6,000	250 years	6½ days	2,700	1

1

The solar system is our own small corner of the universe. It is made up of the sun and all the bodies which revolve around it: the planets and their satellites, asteroids, comets and meteorites.

Size of planets in relation to the sun:

1 Mercury
2 Venus
3 The Earth
4 Mars
5 Jupiter
6 Saturn
7 Uranus
8 Neptune

The history
of the solar system

If you look at the sky from the Earth, it seems as though the Earth stays still, with the sun moving round it. Ptolemy, an astronomer who lived in the first century AD, worked out a system more or less fitting these observations. The Earth was in the middle of the universe, with the sun, the planets and the stars moving around it, each fixed in its own transparent sphere, each sphere

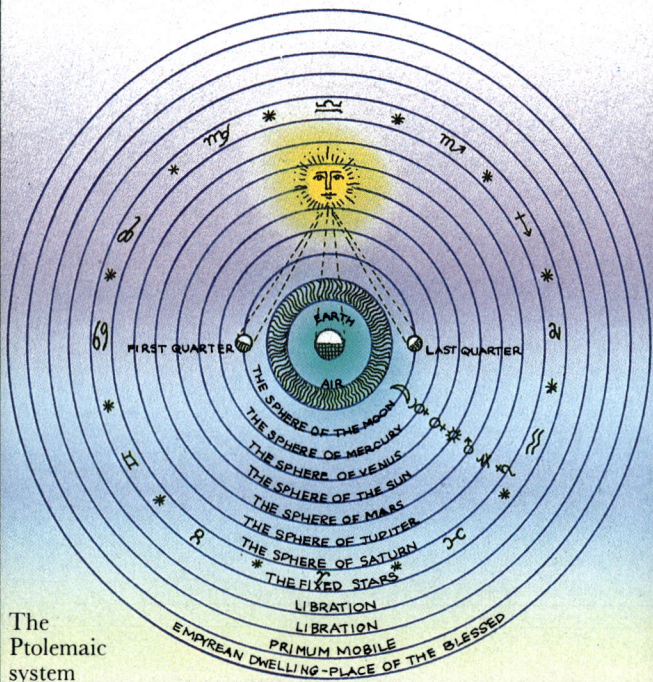

FIRST QUARTER   EARTH   LAST QUARTER

AIR

THE SPHERE OF THE MOON
THE SPHERE OF MERCURY
THE SPHERE OF VENUS
THE SPHERE OF THE SUN
THE SPHERE OF MARS
THE SPHERE OF JUPITER
THE SPHERE OF SATURN
THE FIXED STARS
LIBRATION
LIBRATION
PRIMUM MOBILE
EMPYREAN DWELLING-PLACE OF THE BLESSED

The
Ptolemaic
system

revolving at a different pace. But Ptolemy's explanation did not fit all the observations.

In the sixteenth century a Polish scholar, Copernicus, found he could solve this problem by thinking of the planets as revolving, not around the Earth, but around the sun, with the Earth just another planet among them. Modern astronomy was born.

Copernicus

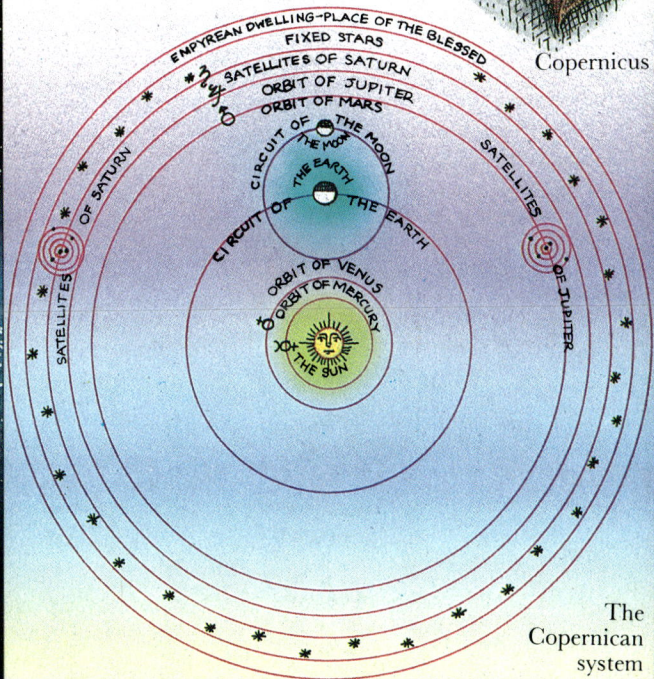

The Copernican system

The planets

The stars shine by themselves; planets only reflect the sun's light. Nowadays we have identified nine planets which revolve around our sun, although only five of them are visible to the naked eye.

Mercury The planet closest to the sun, small (hardly bigger than our moon), and without an atmosphere to protect it from the sun's radiation, Mercury is a harsh, inhospitable rocky world. By day temperatures may reach 400°C, by night they can go down to −200°C. Mercury is quite hard to see from Earth with the naked eye.

Venus Even more inhospitable. Almost as large as the Earth, it is our nearest planetary neighbour. A day on Venus is nearly equal to four Earth months. Its atmosphere, composed almost entirely of carbon dioxide, allows the sunlight through but does not let the heat escape — temperatures can rise to 450°C. So far no spacecraft has been able to survive on Venus for more than an hour.

Mars With its changing polar caps, red deserts and green markings, Mars, although half the size of Earth, seemed Earth's twin sister. Space probes, though, have shown that it is more like the moon than the Earth, with no water-vapour in the atmosphere, little water on the surface, and extremes of

Telescope
(25 m diameter)

The surface of
Mercury

Venus

temperature. No trace of life has yet been found on Mars.

The asteroids Between the orbits of Mars and Jupiter are thousands of small bodies rotating in space. They are asteroids, or very small planets. The biggest of them have diameters of below 1,000 km.

Jupiter The largest of the planets, it takes nearly twelve Earth years to orbit the sun, at an average distance from the sun of 750 million km. It is a cold world (−150°C), with an atmosphere composed of hydrogen, helium and ammonia, and much atmospheric turbulence. It is circled by a thin ring.

Saturn Its atmosphere is very similar to that of Jupiter. Its bright lights and its rings have long made it distinctive among Earth's planets. One theory is that these rings are made up from rock fragments of a moon, or moons, which once revolved around Saturn, and broke up when they came too close to the planet.

Uranus and Neptune Both are very distant and difficult to observe. Recently astronomers have found that Uranus has rings.

Pluto Only discovered in 1930. It is tiny, probably smaller than our moon, with an orbit at an angle to the orbits of the other planets.

The red spot on Jupiter, thought to be the eye of a huge and almost permanent storm

A space probe on Mars

Saturn

Comets and meteorites

After William the Conqueror sailed over from Normandy and, defeating Harold, became King of England in 1066, the events of the conquest were woven into a long tapestry called the Bayeux Tapestry. In the tapestry there is a star which appeared in April 1066 and was taken as a warning of Harold's doom — 'a new star, a new king' was the saying. In fact, it wasn't a star, but one of the brightest and most predictable of the solar system's comets, Halley's Comet.

What comets are is still not fully understood, though astronomers know a lot about what they do.

A bright comet usually consists of four parts: the cloud-like head, or *coma*; the bright, star-like centre, or *nucleus*; the *tail*; and a very faint surrounding cloud of *hydrogen*.

A comet moves in a *parabolic orbit*, with its tail always pointing away from the sun. (You can get an idea of the shape of a parabolic orbit by swinging a ball around on a string, altering the length of the string as the ball goes round. If the ball is a comet, your hand is the sun.)

Halley's Comet takes about 75 years to complete its orbit. The next sighting of it will be in 2060.

ISTI MIRANT STELLA

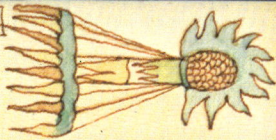

Comets are not the only small bodies which travel through space and through our solar system. Other fragments of dust and rock appear regularly in the sky, and sometimes even penetrate the Earth's atmosphere to fall to the ground. These are meteors, meteorites, and fireballs.

Some meteors ('shooting stars') orbit together through space, re-appearing in the night sky at regular intervals. One such meteor 'shower' is the Perseids, which makes a spectacular display every August.

Larger fragments of rock or iron sometimes get caught in the Earth's gravitational field and fall on to the surface of the planet. When they land, they are called meteorites. Although the burning gases surrounding them look very dramatic, meteorites are quite small and rarely do any harm. Sometimes, though, the burning gases can cause fires — in Siberia in 1908, a meteorite falling in a forest burned a patch 60 km in diameter.

Halley's Comet as shown in the Bayeux Tapestry (eleventh century). The sentence in Latin means 'They admire the star'.

Iron meteorite

Stone meteorite

Crater caused by a falling meteorite in Arizona

Nebulae and galaxies

The Andromeda nebula

If you are observing the sky on a clear night, you will notice, strung across the sky, areas of misty light, which are very difficult to make out in any detail. These are called *nebulae* — the word means indistinct and hard to get hold of.

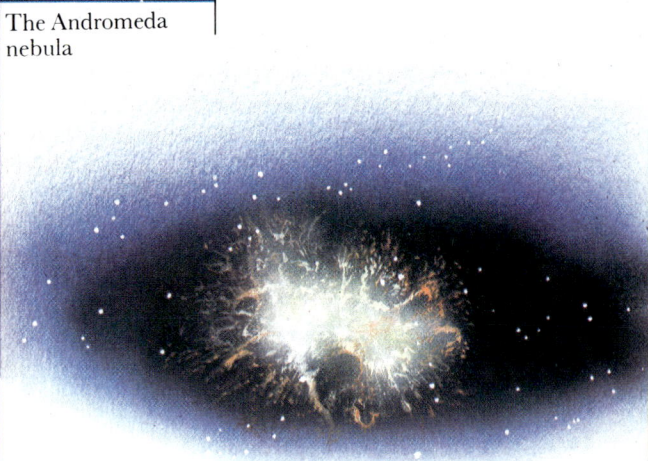

The Crab nebula

Though they all look similar from Earth, there are in fact two sorts of nebula. Those close to us, within our own galaxy, are clouds of dust and gas. Sometimes, if it does not have a nearby star to light it up, a nebula will not shine. It will, in fact, only be visible because of the way in which it cuts out the light of the stars beyond it. The Coal Sack is a nebula like this.

More distant nebulae, however, such as the Andromeda nebula and the Hunting Dogs nebula, are in fact enormous galaxies and star-systems; they only appear luminous and cloud-like because they are so far away.

Most nebulae in our own galaxy are clouds of collapsing gas and dust in which stars are being born. Others have their origin in stars which have exploded and flung their fragments of rock outwards. Gradually, as the centuries pass, the fragments are dispersing.

The Crab nebula, for instance, is the remains of a star which Chinese astronomers observed exploding in 1054. As it exploded it became so bright that it was clearly visible, even by daylight, for over a year.

Our galaxy:

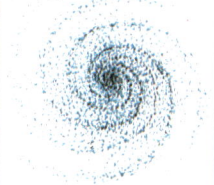

from the front

from the side

The Hunting Dogs galaxy

Slowly, silently, now the moon
Walks the night in her silver shoon;
This way, and that, she peers, and sees
Silver fruit upon silver trees;
One by one the casements catch
Her beams beneath the silvery thatch;
Couched in his kennel, like a log,
With paws of silver sleeps the dog;
From their shadowy cote the white
breasts peep
Of doves in a silver-feathered sleep;
A harvest-mouse goes scampering by,
With silver claws, and silver eye;
And moveless fish in the water gleam,
By silver reeds in a silver stream.

Walter de la Mare

The moon

The moon is our companion body, or *satellite*, travelling around the Earth as the Earth travels round the sun.

It is a small, barren world, with no atmosphere and no water. It takes 27.3 days to orbit the Earth, and exactly the same length of time to rotate upon its axis, so that it always presents the same side to us. The moon gives off no light of its own — moonlight is light from the sun being reflected off the moon's surface.

You can see from the picture how the changing pattern of light and shadows caused by the changing positions of moon, Earth and sun creates the regular growth and contraction of light on the moon's surface which we call the *phases of the moon*.

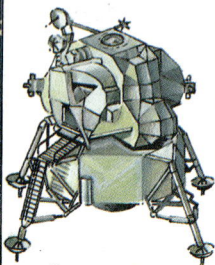

Apollo

Neil Armstrong's footprints

'One small step for a man; a giant leap for mankind.' (Armstrong's words as he stepped on to the moon)

Our satellite is so close to us, a bare 385,000 km away, that its main features have been known for a long time. Even with the naked eye, if you look carefully at the full moon, you can see it is not a smooth surface, but covered in patterns and patches.

The invention of the telescope made it possible to observe the moon quite clearly. Astronomers soon discovered that it was made up of two main areas — 'continents' and 'seas'. In the continents there are mountains and deep craters, most caused by falling meteorites. As early as 1610 Galileo had been able to calculate the height of some of the mountains on the moon. The 'seas' are, of course, not seas, and never have been — they are hard, bare lakes of solid lava, covered with a fine dust.

On 20 July 1969 the American Neil Armstrong, closely followed by his compatriot, Edwin Aldrin, became the first man to walk on the moon. Because there is no atmosphere, no wind, no rain, any mark made on the surface of the moon stays there through the ages — and so Armstrong's footprints will remain for millions of years.

Earthrise

The division of the year into twelve months, first observed by the Mesopotamians, was thought to be in accordance with the pattern underlying the regulation of the physical world. Twelve, and multiples of twelve, became mystic, magic numbers. We still divide circles into 360 degrees, for instance.

The moon's surface (visible face)

Pythagorus
SEA OF COLD
Plato
Aristotle
SEA OF RAINS
Archimedes
THE CAUCASUS
SEA OF SERENITY
THE CARPATHIANS
THE APENNINES
Galileo
OCEAN OF STORMS
Kepler
Copernicus
SEA OF VAPOURS
SEA OF CRISES
SEA OF TRANQUILLITY
Flammarion
Ptolemy
Gutenberg
SEA OF FERTILITY
SEA OF HUMOURS
SEA OF CLOUDS
SEA OF NECTAR
Newton

The sun

You must always take great precautions when observing the sun. Never look at it directly — the brightness of the sun's light can permanently damage your eyes.

Without the energy given out by the sun, life could never have begun and could not survive on Earth. As a star, however, it is relatively small, faint and cool. It appears so huge and hot to us because it is so close — 150 million km. The next nearest star is 300,000 times further away.

The sun has four main areas. At the centre is a huge ball of burning *hydrogen*, surrounded by a skin of dense gas a few hundred miles thick. It is this skin, called the *photosphere*, which gives the sun its even appearance.

Above the photosphere is a more transparent layer called the *chromosphere*. During eclipses you can see huge jets of burning gas shooting out from the chromosphere, making the surface shimmer and dance.

Finally there is the *corona*, a thin cloud of electrons, atoms and dust, so rarefied that it is almost a vacuum. Close to the sun's surface the corona is very hot, but it cools down as it disperses into space.

Eclipses

Lunar eclipse When the moon goes through the shadow cast by the Earth, it disappears from sight, and is no longer lit up. This phenomenon is visible to everyone on Earth for whom it is night at that moment.

Solar eclipse The sun is a great deal larger than the moon, but much further away. Viewed from the Earth, they both appear the same size. If you are standing at just the right spot on the Earth's surface when the moon travels between the Earth and the sun, it will seem to hide the sun completely. Then you can see the sun's corona in all its glory.

Lunar eclipse

Solar eclipse

Myths and legends of the sun

Helios riding the chariot of the sun

Thy dawning is beautiful in the horizon of heaven,
  O living Aton, beginning of life!
All cattle rest upon their herbage,
  All trees and plants flourish,
The birds flutter in their marshes,
Their wings uplifted in adoration to thee.
All the sheep dance upon their feet,
All winged things fly,
They live when thou hast shone upon them.

Akhenaton's Hymn to Aton (the Sun-god)

The sun, as the source of heat and light, has been worshipped by man since earliest times.

Inca temple of the sun

Helios

In Greek myth Helios ('sun' in Greek), his hair streaming fire, would set out in his chariot of gold to ride across the heavens until dusk, when his horses would bathe in the sea.

The peoples of the sun

In Central and South America the Maya, Aztec and Inca peoples built huge pyramids and temples to the sun. They saw the sun as being both good and bad, giving warmth and life to their crops, but also bringing drought and disaster. It was a god to be celebrated, but also to be pacified.

Nut

The Egyptians pictured the sky as a goddess stretched over them. Her brother, Geb, was the Earth, and their father, Shu, the atmosphere.

Hathor

At first Hathor was seen as the goddess of the sky, but later Egyptians saw her as the great mother goddess. She was often depicted as a cow.

Re and Aton

The Egyptians had different names for the sun as it appeared at different times: Khepri was the rising sun, Atum the setting sun, Re the sun at its height, and Aton the sun's disc.

Nut

The goddess Hathor

The god Re

Why the sky is blue

When the weather's fine, the sky arches an unbroken blue overhead. At dusk, it gradually glows red around the sinking sun. In the night it is so dark a blue it seems almost black.

Why should the sky change colour?

Of all the wonders around us, the air is perhaps the most miraculous — it gives us life, and yet we cannot see it. Not only does it give us life by providing the mixture we need to breathe; it was because there was an atmosphere clinging around our world that life was able to develop in the first place, protected from the sun's radiation and from all the dust and particles of space. No planet can sustain life without an atmosphere — think of Mercury, and the dusty, lifeless plains of the moon. Our atmosphere, our air, filters the sun's energy for us and makes it beneficial.

It is a shield we cannot see — or think we cannot. But it is in fact the air that we see when we watch the changing colours of the sky — or rather, not the air itself, for its gases, its particles of dust and moisture are too small for our eyes, but we see the sun's light reflected on each of these particles; depending on the angle at which the sun's rays strike them, and depending on how much moisture there is in the air, so the sky seems to change colour.

The light from the sun is not one colour, but all the colours of the rainbow.

All these colours, from ultra-violet to infra-red, combine together to appear white. But each of these colours is a light-wave sent from the sun, and the different colours are light-waves of different length. When the sun is high in the sky on a fine day, more of the long light-waves, the blues and violets, get through the atmosphere, while the shorter reddish-orange rays bounce off the particles in the air and are reflected back into space. It is because so much ultra-violet gets through on a sunny day, particularly in summer when the sun is highest in the sky, that you must be careful sunbathing — ultra-violet is the most damaging of the sun's rays and can burn you badly. As the earth turns, though, the angle of the light coming from the sun towards the earth changes, and as evening approaches more and more of the sun's blue rays bounce off the air's particles, while more and more of the red rays get through. Eventually, the sun goes entirely out of sight, and we get no more direct light — only, on moonlit nights, the sun's light reflected off our moon. And, of course, the light from other suns — our stars.

How air moves . . .

It is the upward and downward movement of masses of air, changing temperature as they move, which creates wind and forms the clouds.

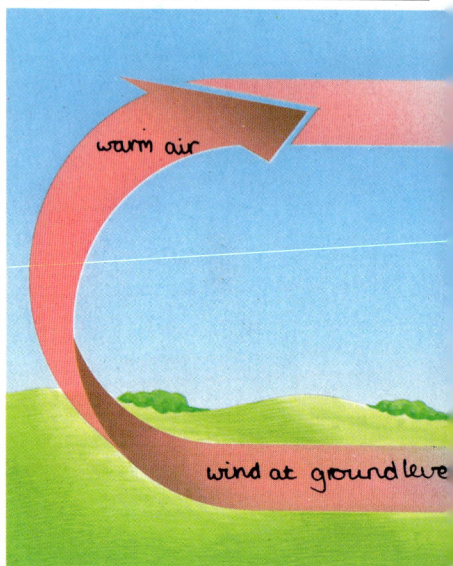

A mass of cold air cannot contain as much humidity as a mass of warm air.

The difference is significant: at 0°C, a cubic metre of air can only hold 5 g of water vapour, while at 30°C, it can hold 30 g. Hot air cools as it rises, and there comes a point when it has to shed its excess load of humidity. The condensation caused by this humidity gives rise to a cloud.

. . . and clouds are formed

Air circulating over a plain

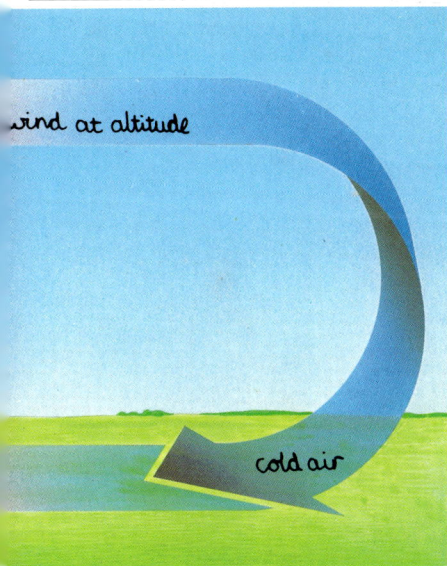

wind at altitude

cold air

Air circulating over a mountain, with the current of air following the slope of the mountain, pushed up by the breeze rising from the valley floor. It cools down at a rate of about 1°C per 100m of elevation. Once it has passed the summit, it can go back down towards the ground, warming up as it goes, and arrive back at ground level drier and hotter than when it started.

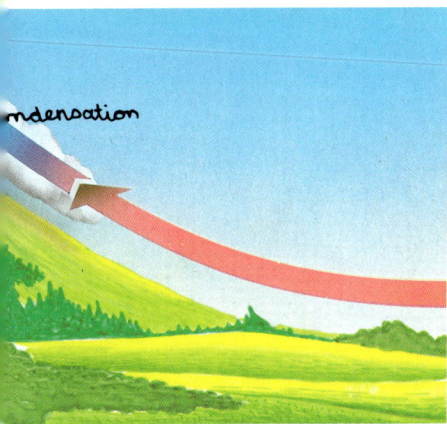

condensation

Clouds

1 Cirrus
2 Alto-stratus
3 Alto-cumulus
4 Strato-cumulus
5 Stratus
6 Cirro-stratus
7 Nimbo-stratus
8 Cumulo-nimbus
9 Cumulus

Clouds are classified mainly according to their shape and their altitude. Thin layers of cloud are *stratus*; streaks of cloud, *cirrus*; and fluffy clouds, *cumulus*. The prefix *cirro-* indicates clouds at over 6,000 m altitude, while *alto-* indicates clouds between 2,000 m and 6,000 m. Finally, *cumulo-nimbus* develop vertically. They are thunder-clouds.

ice crystals

hail

hail

descending currents

descending currents

fine hailstones

56

precipitation   large hailstones

direction of storm

Inside a storm-cloud

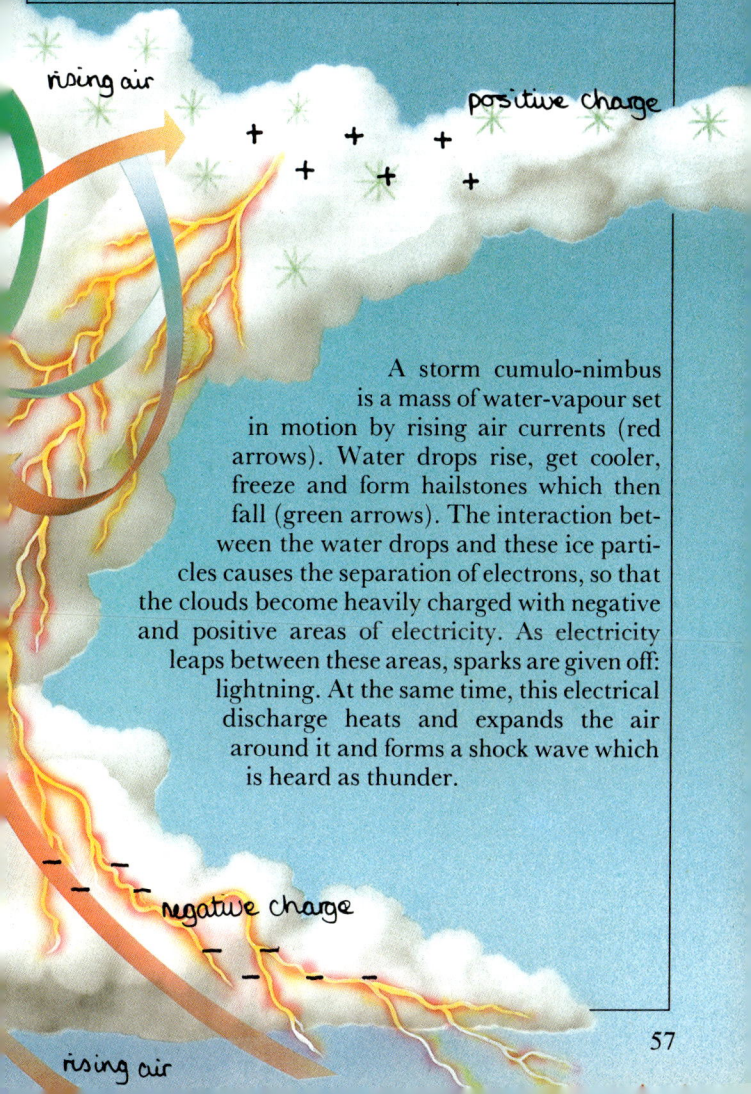

rising air

positive charge

A storm cumulo-nimbus
is a mass of water-vapour set
in motion by rising air currents (red
arrows). Water drops rise, get cooler,
freeze and form hailstones which then
fall (green arrows). The interaction between the water drops and these ice particles causes the separation of electrons, so that
the clouds become heavily charged with negative
and positive areas of electricity. As electricity
leaps between these areas, sparks are given off:
lightning. At the same time, this electrical
discharge heats and expands the air
around it and forms a shock wave which
is heard as thunder.

negative charge

rising air

1

3

4

58

5

The water cycle

There are about 1,500 million cubic km of water on Earth. Most of it (99%) is in the oceans and frozen in the polar caps. The rest is in lakes and rivers, in the ground and in the air.

1 Condensation
2 Evaporation
3 Rain
4 Rivers
5 Underground streams

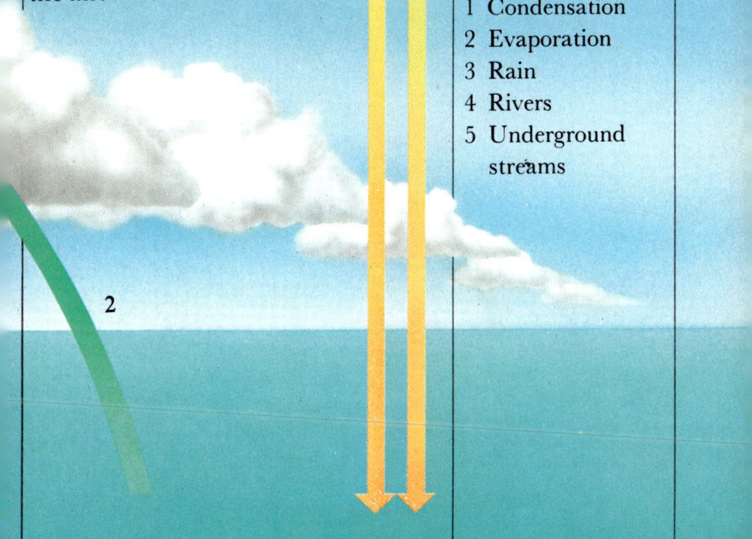

2

The water in the atmosphere comes from the evaporation of the oceans caused by the heat of the sun. The condensation of this water vapour forms clouds and generates rain, hail and snow.

The wind

Wind is a huge draught. It is air moving, and this movement is set off by differences in temperature and changes in pressure.

Some parts of the ground absorb and retain the sun's heat more than others. This means that different areas lose the heat at different rates, and so heat up the air over them at different rates. During the day, air over a road is warmer than the air over a nearby river, and the air over a beach warmer than out at sea.

As the air is heated up, the gases in the air expand and it becomes lighter and rises upward. As it does so, cooler air moves in underneath and takes its place. For instance, if you're sitting on a beach on a hot day, you will notice the breeze blowing in from the sea. The cooler air from over the sea is moving in to take the place of the air which has been heated up by warmth rising from the beach, and which has risen upwards. At night-time, on the other hand, the sea retains the sun's heat longer than the land, and so the breeze moves in the other direction, with the cooler air from the land replacing the warm air which has risen upwards over the sea.

Larger currents of moving air are caused by differences in pressure in the atmosphere, and by the rotation of the earth as it drags the air around with it. Different temperatures around the Earth also cause the wind to blow in particular directions; for example, the air over the poles is cooler than the air round the equator, and the air over the oceans cooler than the air over the continents.

So the Earth has regular predictable winds as well as small local unpredictable ones.

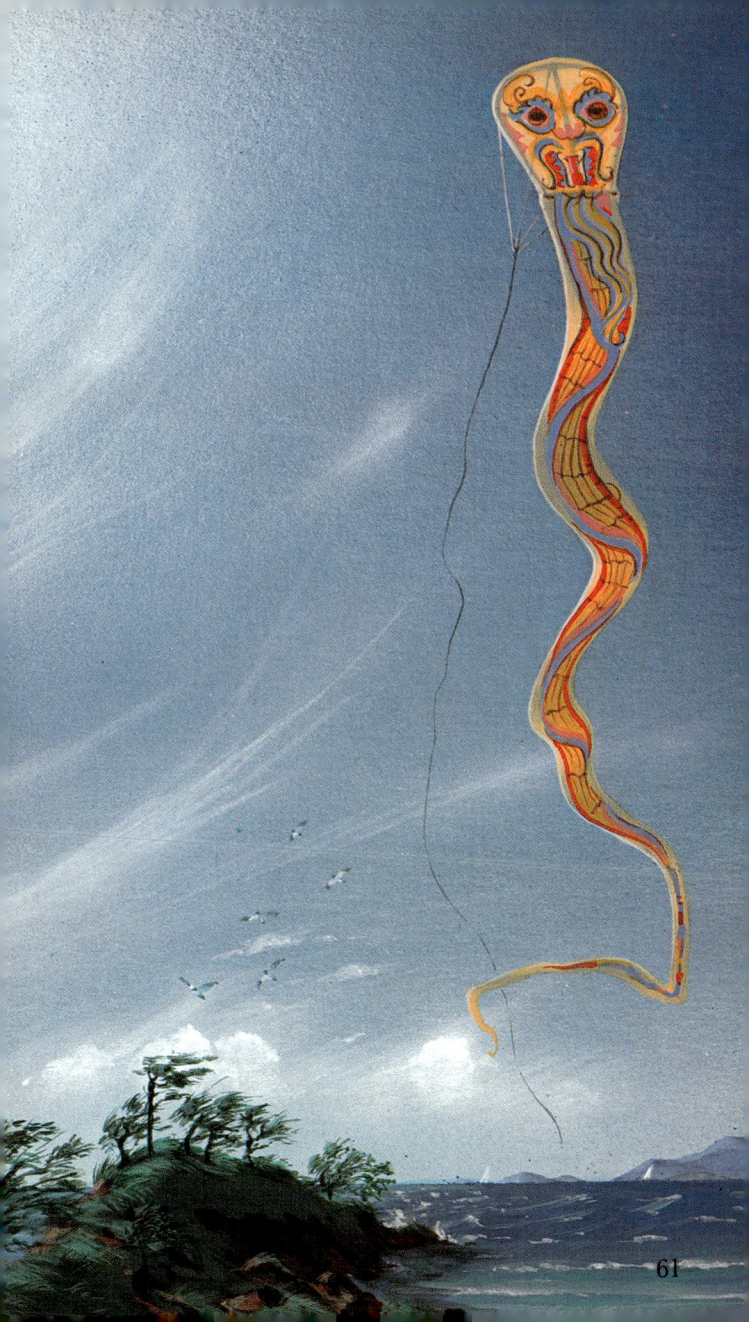

Mountain breezes and . . .

Mountain breeze by day Under the sun's heat, the mountain warms up more rapidly than the valley. The air moves from the valley towards the mountain top.

Mountain breeze by night The mountain cools down faster than the valley. The air moves downwards.

. . . sea breezes

Sea breeze by day The land warms up more rapidly than the water. As warm air rises over the coast it is replaced by cold air from over the sea; the breeze blows from the sea towards the land.

Sea breeze by night The sea retains the heat, the land cools down. The warm air over the sea rises; the breeze blows from the land towards the sea.

Warm fronts, cold fronts

mass of warm air

mass of cold air

Fronts are the point where two air masses with different temperatures meet. Above, you can see a *cold front*: cold air is pushing in under the warm air mass.

Below, a *warm front*: the warm air is sliding over the cold air.

warm air

cool air

Cold air invades warm air Cold air suddenly encounters warm air which cools down rapidly. Thick clouds form. The bad weather doesn't last long.

Cold air meets cold air Sometimes, when a cold front gets close to a cool front, the mass of warmer air separating the two cold masses rises, and the masses of cold air meet. When that happens, there is heavy rainfall at the point where they come together.

The passage . . .

The next 6 pages will show you the progress of a depression over 24 hours.

In our latitudes, depressions — areas of low pressure — moving in from the west bring bad weather. If the depression is very extended and slow-moving, the bad weather may last several days.

At sunset

The sky is blue, the air is still. The last few fine-weather cumulus clouds have just disappeared. It is warm: 17°C. It looks as if it will be fine next day. But high up in the blue sky, a few ragged cirrus clouds are forming. Almost imperceptibly, the barometer begins to fall.

. . . of a depression

The next morning The sun is surrounded by a luminous halo. It is hedged in with cirro-stratus. A south wind has risen. The barometer is falling rapidly. Birds fly in from far out at sea towards the land. The battle between cold air and warm air is on.

During the day

Now the sky is covered with alto-cumulus, a flock of fluffy, iron-grey clouds. The barometer plummets. The temperature rises: 19°C. The sea begins to get restless.

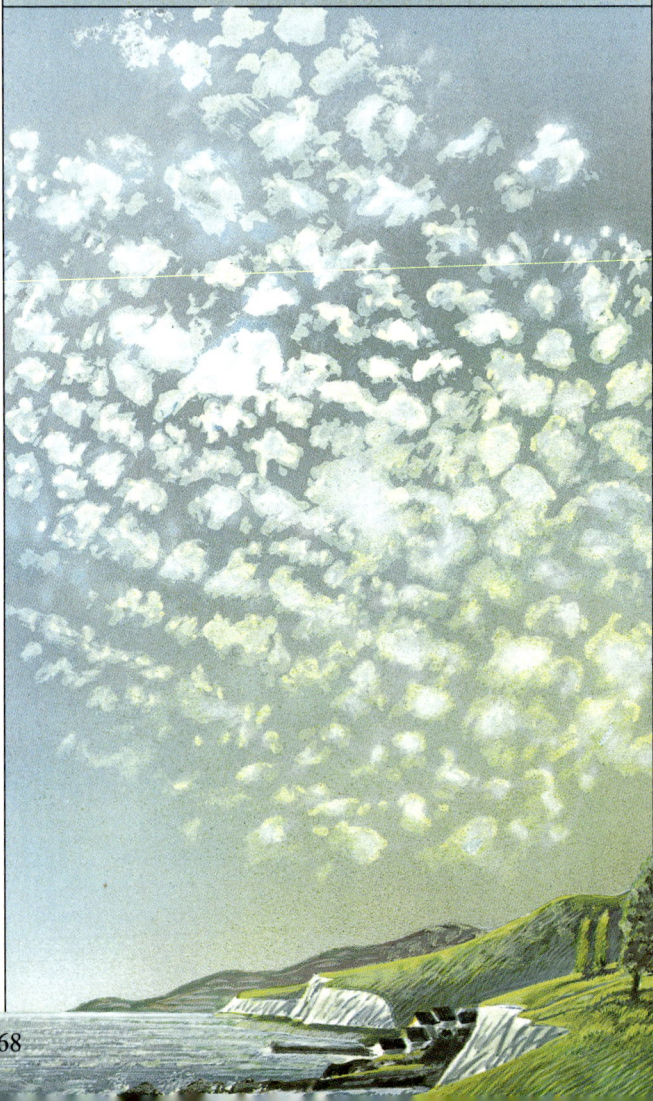

The centre of the depression has arrived. The sky is covered with nimbus and nimbo-stratus. The sea rises, the wind blows hard and rain falls violently. The barometer reaches its lowest point.

During the evening The storm has passed. The barometer is rising slowly. First big cumulus, then stratocumulus clouds form. The temperature goes down: 16°C. The wind starts to settle, though there are still occasional gusts.

The struggle between warm air and cold air is over. Fair-weather cumulus clouds reappear. Maybe another depression is approaching. Maybe the weather is set fair. The rainbow seems a good sign.

Meteorology

1 A warm front

2 A cold front

A Anticyclone

D Depression

Isobars (curves of the same pressure)

Weather maps are drawn up using information sent in from weather stations all over the world. The drawing below shows an imaginary chart which will help you to read and understand the weather maps you see in newspapers and on television.

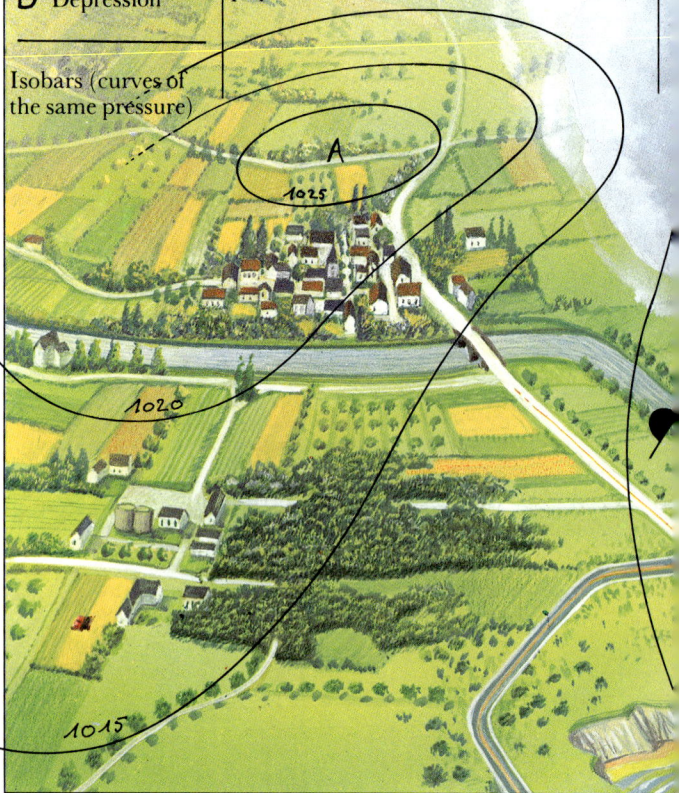

The village on the left is under an anticyclone (A). The weather is fine and the sky is clear. The city on the right is experiencing a depression (D).

The depression was preceded by a warm front (1): cloudy sky, stormy rain. Now the cold front (2) is dominant: showers and gusty wind.

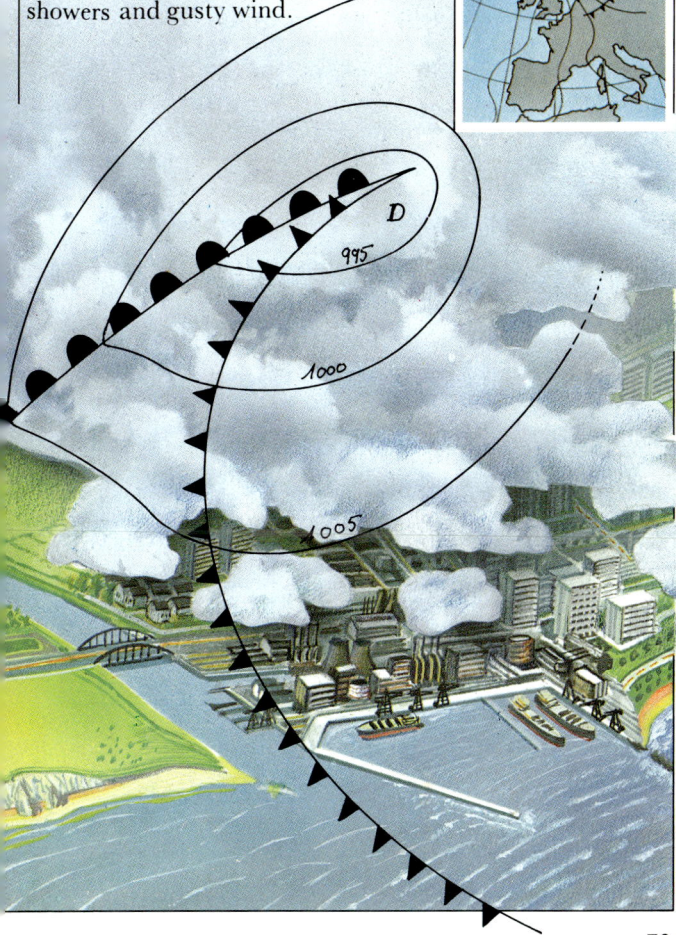

D

995

1000

1005

Thunder and lightning

Dangerpoints:

an isolated tree

a tentpole,
a metal tool

a corrugated
iron shelter

After a hot day, when the air is heavy with humidity, there are often thunderstorms.

Inside a rising column of cumulonimbus, falling particles of ice meet warm air rising. The electrons separate, and electrical charges leap back and forth between the areas of positive and negative charge. The air is alive with the flashes and the explosive sound of the shock waves travelling through the air — we see the flashes first because light travels more quickly than sound.

You must be very careful where you take shelter in a thunderstorm. The electricity being discharged in the lightning flashes will seek the quickest and easiest route to the earth. The air is, in fact, quite a poor conductor of electricity, so that a tree, a building, a fence-post, all present more attractive routes for the lightning. If you are caught in a thunderstorm, stay in the open – it is better to get wet than to be struck by lightning.

Blow, winds, and crack your cheeks! rage! blow!
You cataracts and hurricanoes, spout ...
... And thou, all-shaking thunder,
Strike flat the thick rotundity o' the world!

William Shakespeare

Cyclones, hurricanes, tornadoes

Cyclones and anticyclones are the circular movements of the air. Hurricanes and tornadoes occur when these movements become violent, frightening and destructive.

Hurricanes begin over the sea near the equator. The local air-currents suck up water-vapour, each current twisting round the others in a counter-clockwise spiral. New moist air from outside, together with the heat discharged from the condensing vapour within, increase the wind's violence. A full-grown hurricane may have winds of 300 km/h, while the still 'eye' at its

1 The eye of the hurricane
2 Direction of winds and currents
3 Wall round the eye

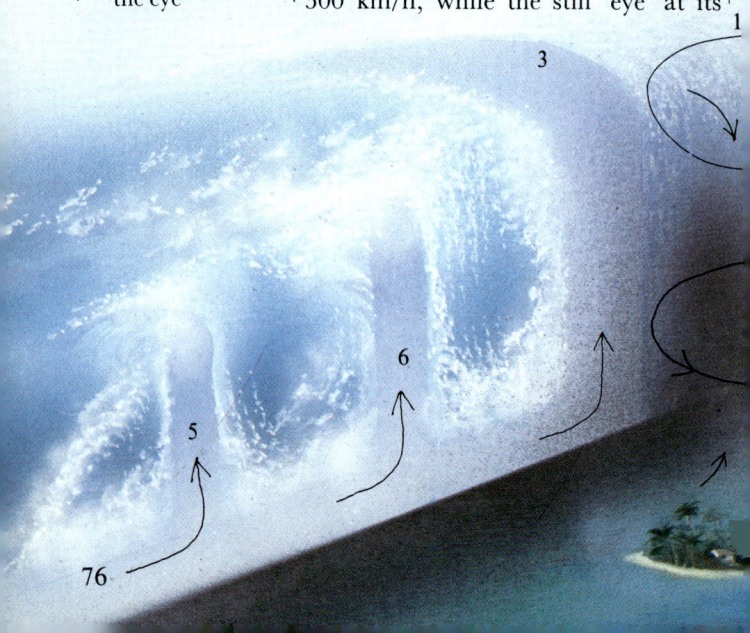

centre may measure 48 km across.

Tornadoes, the most frightening storms of all, occur when a mass of warm air trapped within a mass of cold air corkscrews violently upwards, wrapping the cold air around it so that a huge, twisting funnel is formed. As the tornado travels along, it snatches up everything in its path — rain, dust, clouds, trees, cars, the roofs of houses, all being whirled around at speeds up to 500 km/h. At the same time, the low pressure inside the tornado may literally explode buildings outwards, because of the higher pressure within them.

4 Direction of winds at the summit

5,6,7,8 Rising currents

9 Convergence of winds towards the centre

10 Evacuation

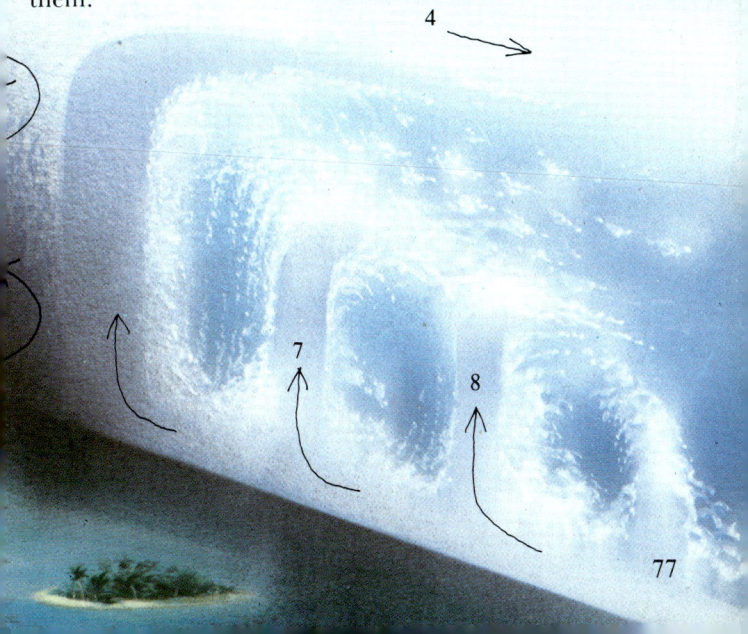

The rainbow

When the air is full of water-vapour after a rain shower, and then the sky clears and the sun comes out, you will often see a rainbow in the sky opposite the sun.

Each drop of vapour acts as a tiny prism, breaking up the light.

The sun's light is refracted by all the tiny drops of water and is broken up into the separate colours of the spectrum.

Water the garden as the sun sinks on a clear day and you may see rainbows.

I do set my bow in the cloud . . . The bow shall be in the cloud; and I will look upon it, that I may remember the everlasting covenant between God and every living creature of all flesh that is upon the Earth.

Genesis, 9, vv. 13-16

Aureoles, haloes and parahelions

As well as rainbows, light can cause other phenomena in the atmosphere.

Aureoles Sometimes, on a slightly cloudy day, when the sun is low in the sky, you may see a tree, or perhaps someone you're talking to, surrounded by a circle of rainbow-coloured light: the sun is throwing their shadows on to a cloud.

Aureole |

80

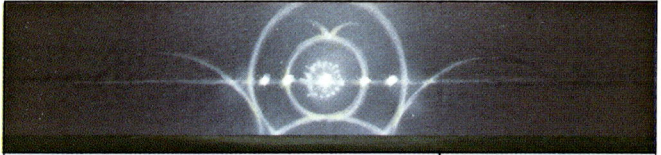

Parahelion A very rare phenomenon, when the sun appears to be surrounded by lots of lesser, false suns, linked to it by bridges of light.

Haloes Sometimes, on a misty day, you may see a halo round the sun or moon. This is often a sign of bad weather, because the halo is not caused by the mist, but by small ice particles in a fine layer of cirrus cloud.

Parahelion

Halo

Aurora borealis: the northern lights

Perhaps the most dramatic of all the phenomena visible in our atmosphere are the auroras which can be seen at the North and South Poles, with their gleaming sheets of purple, green and gold lighting up the night sky. The auroras are not in fact due to the action of light on the atmosphere, but to parti-

Aurora australis: the southern lights

cles ejected by the sun and caught in the Earth's magnetic field. The Earth as a whole is a huge magnet, with the ends, as it were, passing through the Poles. The particles from the sun are held in this magnetic field and discharge their light in a fantastic display of dancing colours.

Some rays of the aurora may reach 1,000 km high.

The sun descending in the west,
The evening star does shine;
The birds are silent in their nest,
And I must seek for mine.
The moon, like a flower
In heaven's high bower,
With silent delight
Sits and smiles on the night.

William Blake

A dictionary of the sky

the altitude of stars. Perfected by Arab and Persian astronomers between the 9th and 11th centuries.

Atom

The smallest known particle or quantity possessing identifiable characteristics.

Aerolite

Literally a 'stone of the air', meteorite.

Anemometer

Instrument for measuring the force of the wind.

Angstrom unit

Measurement of the wavelength of light. 1 ångstrom = 1/10,000,000 mm.

Anticyclone

A region of atmospheric high pressure giving rise to good weather.

Asteroids

Name given to the small planetary bodies revolving round the sun between Mars and Jupiter.

Astrolabe

An instrument formerly used to measure

Barometer

Instrument for the measurement of atmospheric pressure.

Binaries

Stars that move together in pairs.

Bissextile (year)

Name given to the year occurring every 4 years in which February has 29 days. Leap year.

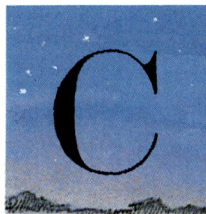

Celestial sphere

The early Greeks thought that the sky was like an upturned bowl, a shield protecting the Earth from surrounding fires. The stars were holes in the bowl through which the flames could be seen.

Copernicus

Nicholaus Copernicus, 1473-1543. Polish astronomer. His work on the structure of the solar system opened the way for such founders of modern astronomy as Galileo, Tycho Brahe, Kepler and Newton.

Cosmic rays

Particles, mainly protons, with tremendously high energies. Thought to be the product of exploding stars, or *supernova*.

Crab nebula

Still expanding, it now measures 400 million million miles across.

Deimos
Second satellite of Mars, discovered in 1877. Only 12 km in diameter.

Draconids
Meteor shower visible at the end of the first week in October.

Einstein
Albert Einstein, 1879-1955. Mathematical physicist. His theories of relativity explained many puzzles in the movement of light and of planets.

Equinox
Date when, all the world over, day and night are of equal length. The spring equinox falls on 20/21 March, the autumn equinox on 22/23 September.

Expanding universe
Theory explaining the evolution of the universe in terms of an initial explosion: the 'big bang' theory.

Flamsteed
John Flamsteed, 1646-1719. First Astronomer Royal. Laid the basis of modern astronomy through his observations of the sun and the movements of the stars.

Galaxy
Concentration of stars sometimes containing several solar systems. The nearest galaxy to our own comparable in size and mass is the Andromeda nebula.

Galileo
Galileo Galilei, 1564-1642. Italian scientist and astronomer. Made many major discoveries and observations. A great follower of Copernicus' sun-centred universe, he was arrested by the Catholic Church as a heretic, and made to declare he thought the theory untrue. He was heard to mutter, even as he did so, '*E pur, si muove*' — 'and yet the Earth *does* move . . .'

Hygrometer
Used to measure humidity in air.

Icarus
Figure from Greek myth. Daedalus, his father, made them both a set of wings in order that they could escape from the Minotaur in Crete. But Icarus, daring and thoughtless, flew too close to the sun. The wax holding his wings together mel-

ted; he fell into the sea, and drowned. An asteroid discovered in 1949 is named after him.

Ionosphere
Layer of Earth's atmosphere 140 km up.

Jupiter
In 1609, using his telescope, Galileo discovered the biggest moons of Jupiter, the four major satellites moving in orbit round the planet, just as the planets orbit the sun.

Kepler
Johann Kepler, 1571-1630. German astronomer. Working on Tycho Brahe's observations, Kepler developed mathematical 'laws' explaining the movements of the planets, and opened the way for Newton's work on gravity.

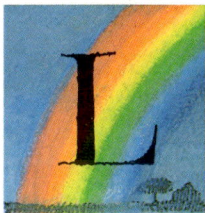

Light
Although light travels very fast (about 300,000 km a second), some of the stars we see through telescopes are so far away that, by the time their light reaches us, the stars themselves may have disappeared.

Lunatic
Name given to people whose changes of mood alter like the phases of the moon.

Magnetic field
Our whole galaxy is probably contained within a huge magnetic bubble. Lines of force seem to be mainly parallel to the plane of the galaxy. Other lines of force may emerge from the centre of the galaxy to surround the entire distribution of stars.

Meteors
Tiny grains of space debris which burn up in a flash as they enter our atmosphere.

Milky Way
Our home galaxy. It is shaped like a pair of fried eggs stuck together on their flat sides, and contains 100,000 million stars — including the sun.

Newton
Sir Isaac Newton, born Christmas Day, 1642, died 1727. Astronomer and mathematician. Discovered how to calculate the orbit of a body moving under a central force — gravity.

Nova

Term given to the sudden appearance of a 'new star' (*stella nova*). Twenty or so novae may be visible to the naked eye in the course of a century.

Orbit

The path followed by one planetary body travelling around another. Kepler showed that, instead of moving in circles, as the ancient astronomers thought, bodies travel in an oval path.

Orion nebula

A dense cloud of gas and dust, in which it is possible to observe newly-formed stars.

Planetarium

A projection-room with a dome-shaped ceiling on to which points of light are projected to demonstrate the movement of the planets and stars.

Poles

Each end, north and south, of the Earth's axis. Also the two points at which the imaginary line of the Earth's axis meets the sky, and so the points around which the stars appear to revolve.

Quasar

Abbreviation of quasi-stellar radiosource. Quasars are the centres of very distant and powerful galaxies. They are extremely energetic — more than

1000 times more powerful than ordinary galaxies.

Radio astronomy

As well as giving out light-waves, bodies in space give out radio-waves of varying 'brightness'. Radio maps of the sky provide astronomers with more information about the universe.

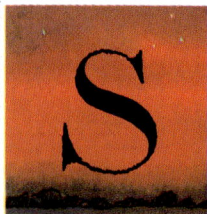

Satellites

Small bodies in orbit round planets. The moon is a satellite of the Earth. There are also artificial, man-made satellites orbiting the Earth, providing information, and services such as communications.

Solar flares

Huge streams of energy emitted from the sun's

corona. Visible at times of total solar eclipse.

Telescopes
Literally meaning 'seeing from a distance', they gather radiation and make distant objects appear closer.

Uranus
At the beginning of the 18th century, it seemed that everything important had been discovered in astronomy. William Herschel's discovery of a new planet, in 1781, came as a bombshell.

Van Allen Belt
Belts of radiation at the Poles recently discovered by space probes.

Willamette
Town in Oregon (USA) famous for a fallen meteor weighing 14 tonnes.

X-rays
Light rays with a very short wave-length but very high energy. This energy is what makes X-rays and, even more, gamma rays, so very dangerous.

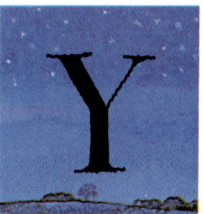

Yerkes Observatory
Williams Bay, USA. One of the world's largest refracting telescopes.

Zenith
The point of the sky directly overhead. In our latitudes, Vega often passes near the zenith during August.

Zodiac
The twelve signs or constellations through which the sun passes in a year:

Capricorn (Dec./Jan.)
Aquarius (Jan./Feb.)
Pisces (Feb./Mar.)
Aries (Mar./Apr.)
Taurus (Apr./May)
Gemini (May/June)
Cancer (June/July)
Leo (July/Aug.)
Virgo (Aug./Sep.)
Libra (Sep./Oct.)
Scorpio (Oct./Nov.)
Sagittarius (Nov./Dec.)

Things to do and to look out for

Observing the stars, and the development of wind and weather, is an absorbing and rewarding occupation.

Watch how clouds change and develop. If you have a camera, perhaps you could take photos of them.

Make notes of what the wind does over a few days. Is it always from the same direction? When does it change? See if you can predict what it will do next.

Look at the moon on a clear night, through binoculars if you have them. Can you see any craters?

Astronomical events to watch out for

Some regular meteor showers visible throughout the world:

Early January	Quadrantids
July/August	Perseids
Mid-October	Orionids
Mid-December	Geminids

Some total eclipses, recent, and to come:

Date	Body	Visible from
28 Oct. 1985	Moon	Australasia, Africa, Asia, Europe, Arctic
17/18 Mar. 1988	Sun	E. Asia, N.W. Australia, extreme N.W. of N. America
20 Feb. 1989	Moon	Arctic, Australasia, Asia, N. America, N.E. Europe
11 Aug. 1999	Sun	Arctic, N. America, Iceland, Europe, N. Africa, Arabia, Asia

In 1985/86 **Halley's Comet** was visible as it passed close to Earth on its 76 year orbit.

In January 1985, the American Voyager 2 space probe flew past Uranus.

Index

The author and
the illustrators

The author of *The Book of the Sky*, **Jean-Pierre Verdet**, is an astronomer at the Paris Observatory. A specialist in Jupiter, Saturn and Mars in particular, he now devotes most of his time to writing books and articles about the history of astronomy.

Christian Broutin illustrated the cover of this book, and pages 6 to 41.

André Rollet illustrated pages 42-9, 54-5, 66-73 and 84.

Isaï Correia illustrated pages 52-3, 56-9 and 62-5.

Christine Adam illustrated pages 74-83.

Jean-Louis Besson has done the vignettes for the Dictionary of the Sky.

Thanks are due to Katherine Matthews for her hand-lettering of the captions.

The editor and publishers wish to thank the following for permission to use copyright material:

Evans Brothers Ltd for *Flying* by J.M. Westrup from Come Follow Me; the Literary Trustees of Walter de la Mare and the Society of Authors as their representative for *Silver* from Collected Rhymes and Verses (Faber & Faber, 1970).